The Moon has [...]
Folk stories [...]
superstitions [...] out your hair,
for instance, [...] have given us the
word 'lunatic' [...] ring is a basic human
desire so on [...] ence and engineering
stretched ou[r] boundary outside Earth's
atmosphere, travelling to our natural
satellite became a challenge.

Helen Sharman, the first Briton
to travel to space, returning
safely from her mission to the
Mir Space Station.

The Moon is the furthest place from Earth
that people have ever set foot. Compared
to the International Space Station, which
is about 400 km above the Earth's surface,
the Moon is much further at around 400,000
km away. There were no guarantees the Apollo
crews would return to Earth safely.

But what an adventure those astronauts had! On the journey, they
experienced a wonderful, free, relaxing feeling of weightlessness.
Views out of the window were awesome, especially when they saw our
distant blue planet rise above the Moon. And just imagine what it
was like to pad about on the dusty surface, bouncing around in one
sixth of the gravity we have on Earth!

Blast Off to the Moon tells you exactly what all that was like.
You can find out how the astronauts ate and what happened to their
food, how the spacecraft worked and what the astronauts did when
they were not busy navigating by the stars. You don't have to read
the book from cover to cover (though you can if you like). You can
dip in and out of the parts that interest you most and come back
to the other sections later.

As space agencies consider using the Moon to get to Mars, people are
applying what we learnt from Apollo to future space missions. Before
I became an astronaut, I would have laughed if anyone suggested I
might go into space. The first Mars crew could include one of your
family and it might even be you. Happy reading!

Helen Sharman

Helen Sharman, Astronaut

Mission to the Moon

"If the mission - called Apollo 11 - is successful, man will accomplish his long-time dream of walking on another celestial body."
- statement of intent from the Apollo 11 Press Kit, 1969

The Apollo 11 mission aimed to land men on the Moon and return them to Earth safely. Once on the Moon, the astronauts would conduct various scientific experiments and collect samples of lunar surface material.

Why did the mission happen?

"We choose to go to the Moon in this decade and do the other things, not because they are easy, but because they are hard." John F. Kennedy

In 1961, President John F. Kennedy vowed that the United States would land a man on the Moon by the end of the 1960s. The result was the Apollo space programme.

The first Apollo mission, Apollo 1, ended in tragedy as all three astronauts were killed in a fire during a test. After extensive redesigning of equipment, the programme resumed. Apollo 11 was the fifth Apollo mission to carry astronauts.

This is a copy of the plaque which the Apollo 11 astronauts left behind on the Moon. It was made of stainless steel and was attached to the landing leg which supported the ladder on the Lunar Module's descent stage.

What did they want to achieve?

The main objective of the Apollo 11 mission was to perform a manned lunar landing and return safely to Earth. The mission also set 11 secondary objectives and five scientific experiments, all of which were completed apart from two (one scientific and one secondary). These investigated the makeup of the Moon and how humans can function when subject to the Moon's unfamiliar conditions. The astronauts also filmed television footage and took photographs, some of which are included in this book.

These illustrations are taken from the Apollo 11 Press Kit. They were created to send out to people before the mission so that they could see what was involved at each stage - from take off to getting the three astronauts home safely. You can find out more about these in the rest of this book!

Astronaut insertion

Check of systems

Saturn staging

Translunar injection

Transposition manoeuvre

Extraction of Lunar Module

Navigation check

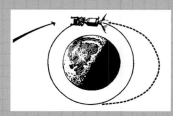
Lunar orbit insertion

Transfer to Lunar Module

Separation of Lunar Module from Command Service Module

Landing on the Moon

First step on the Moon

Commander on the Moon

Collecting samples

Experiment placements

TV camera placement and alignment of passive seismometer

Bulk sample collection

Return to spacecraft and ascent stage launch

Rendezvous and docking

Lunar Module jettison

TransEarth injection

Command Module and Service Module separation

Re-entry and splash down

Recovery

Meet the Astronauts!

Neil, Michael and Buzz posing for a
pre-launch photoshoot

Neil Armstrong, Buzz Aldrin and Michael Collins
were the three astronauts chosen for the Apollo
11 mission. They were all very experienced and had
flown space missions before. Neil was the first
human to actually set foot on the Moon and Buzz
the second. Michael stayed in the Command Module
with the important task of making sure the mission
was a technical success and that his fellow
astronauts were able to return safely.

NAME:	Commander Neil A. Armstrong
JOB:	NASA astronaut
BIRTHDAY:	5 August 1930
BORN:	Wapakoneta, Ohio, USA
DESCRIPTION:	Blond hair, blue eyes, 5 feet 11 inches, 11 stone 11 pounds
EDUCATION:	Attended high school in Wapakoneta and went on to complete a Bachelor of Science degree in Aeronautical Engineering at Purdue University in 1955
FAMILY:	Married to Janet Shearon from Evanston, Illinois and has two children - Eric and Mark
HOBBIES:	Include soaring, for which he is a Federation Aeronautique International gold badge holder
SALARY:	$30,054 a year ($207,000 in 2019)
EXPERIENCE:	He was a naval aviator from 1949-1952 and flew 78 combat missions during the Korean War
RANDOM FACT:	Neil participated in the launch of over 100 rocket aeroplane flights

Neil had a talent and passion for
performance. He wrote and co-directed
two musicals whilst at university,
and played the baritone horn.

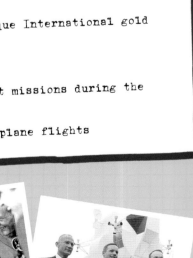

NASA's Apollo 11 astronauts are all smiles having successfully returned
home after being part of one of the greatest moments in history!

NAME:	Lunar Module Pilot Colonel Edwin Eugene 'Buzz' Aldrin Jr.
JOB:	NASA astronaut
BIRTHDAY:	20 January 1930
BORN:	Montclair, New Jersey, USA

Buzz nearly became a sailor and had a place at a naval academy. However, he suffered from seasickness so joined the United States Air Force instead!

DESCRIPTION:	Blond hair, blue eyes, 5 feet 10 inches, 11 stone 11 pounds
EDUCATION:	Attended Montclair High School in New Jersey and went on to complete a Doctor of Science degree in Astronautics at the Massachusetts Institute of Technology in 1963. He also received an Honorary Doctorate of Science degree from Gustavus Adolphus College in 1967
FAMILY:	Married to Joan A. Archer from Ho-Ho-Kus, New Jersey and has three children – Michael, Janice and Andrew
HOBBIES:	Include running, scuba diving and high bar exercises
SALARY:	$18,622.56 a year ($128,265 in 2019)
EXPERIENCE:	He flew 66 combat missions during the Korean War. He also served as an aerial gunnery instructor in Alabama and a flight commander in Germany
RANDOM FACT:	Buzz was a Scout Merit Badge Counsellor

NAME:	Command Module Pilot Colonel Michael Collins
JOB:	NASA astronaut
BIRTHDAY:	31 October 1930
BORN:	Rome, Italy

After his career as an astronaut, Michael became the third director of the Smithsonian National Space and Air Museum in Washington DC, from 1971 to 1978.

DESCRIPTION:	Brown hair, brown eyes, 5 feet 11 inches, 11 stone 11 pounds
EDUCATION:	Attended Saint Albans School in Washington and went on to complete a Bachelor of Science degree from the United States Military Academy, New York in 1952
FAMILY:	Married to Patricia M. Finnegan from Boston, Massachusetts and has three children – Kathleen, Ann and Michael
HOBBIES:	Include fishing and handball
SALARY:	$17,147.36 a year ($118,105 in 2019)
EXPERIENCE:	He served as an experimental flight test officer and has logged more than 4,000 hours flying time
RANDOM FACT:	Michael completed two spacewalks during an earlier NASA mission

Training

How do you prepare for something that has never been done before?
Neil, Buzz and Michael had to undergo more than 1,000 hours of intensive
training before they could set off on their historic journey to the Moon.
This ensured that in the months leading up to the mission,
every second was practised over and over again.

The Apollo 11 astronauts trained alongside their backup crew - Jim Lovell,
Fred Haise and Bill Anders - up until a few weeks before the launch. They
learnt essential space survival skills, such as how to land the lunar module
and manoeuvre in low and zero gravity conditions, as well as geology and
rehearsing putting up the American flag. They also learnt how to withstand
a much greater force of gravity (g force) than you would normally feel
standing on Earth. This was something the astronauts experienced during
launch and had to prepare for to ensure that they
didn't pass out.

They trained indoors, outdoors, in spacesuits,
underwater and in any other condition NASA thought
beneficial. The crew also took part in spacecraft

manufacturing and launch area testing to provide a thorough operational
knowledge of the spacecraft. Contingency plans were also prepared for:
although Apollo 11 was designed to land in the ocean, the astronauts
received jungle and desert survival training in case they hit land instead.

Training aimed to replicate lunar conditions as much as possible on planet
Earth with no definitive proof of what the surface of the Moon was like. Detailed simulators of the
spacecraft and lunar surface were built to give the astronauts as much experience as possible.

In the photo above on the left, you can see Buzz practicing the Solar Wind Composition experiment
during a training session. This took place on a mock up of the lunar surface in Building 9 at the
Manned Spacecraft Center in Houston, Texas.

In the photo above on the right, Neil and Buzz are studying rock
samples whilst on a geological field trip to the Quitman Mountains
in Texas. The Texan desert was chosen for having a theorised
similar geological makeup to the Moon. Here, the astronauts
practiced collecting Moon rock samples using special lunar
geological tools. Whilst Buzz and Neil rehearsed various lunar
surface procedures, Michael practised various manoeuvres for
his time alone in the Command Module. In the photo on the left,
you can see him down beyond the couches with the navigation
equipment to his back in the Command Module simulator.

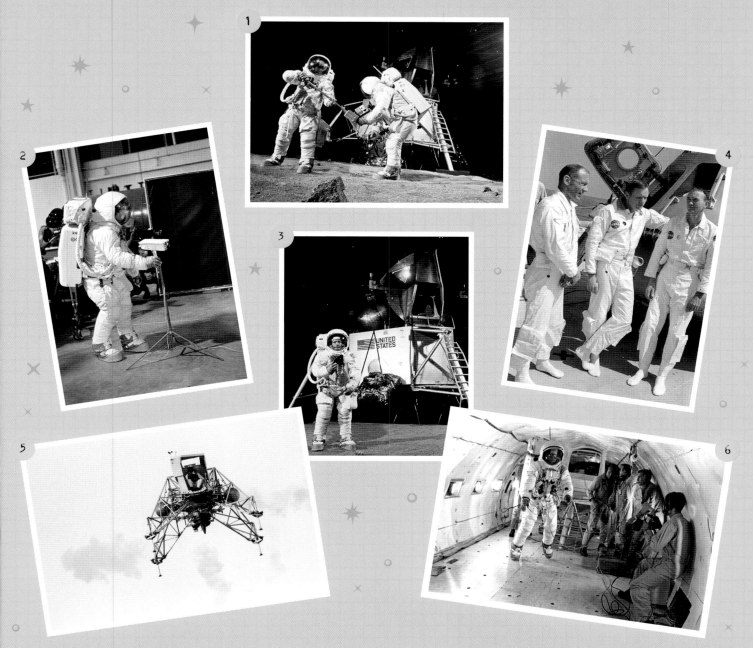

In the photos above, you can see a
range of the different things the three Apollo 11
astronauts had to complete as part of their training:

1: Buzz and Neil practice collecting lunar samples on a mock up of the Moon surface.
   Buzz uses a scoop to collect the sample, whilst Neil holds a bag to receive it.
2: Neil sets up a lunar surface television camera during lunar surface simulation training.
3: Neil practices photographing the lunar surface. The Lunar Module simulator is behind him.
4: Buzz, Neil and Michael relax on the deck of the NASA Motor Vessel Retriever before taking
   part in a training exercise in the Gulf of Mexico to prepare for the ocean landing
   (also known as water egress) planned for their splash down back to Earth.
5: Neil flies the Lunar Landing Training Vehicle in a simulation of landing the Lunar Module.
6: Buzz gets used to weightless conditions on a KC-135 aircraft, which can mimic zero gravity.

Before the Launch

Preparations for the launch began five days beforehand. Tasks during this period included the mechanical build-up of the Command Service Module and Lunar Module, fuel cell activation and servicing and loading helium aboard the Lunar Module.

The Day before the Launch

The official launch countdown started at T-28 hours, the day before the launch date. T-xx, pronounced 'T minus', meant the time before the scheduled launch time of 9.32 am EDT (Eastern Daylight Time – the timezone used in Florida, where the launch took place) on 16 July 1969. This involved the build-up and loading of the rocket and spacecraft and pre-launch checks. One essential task was to load the huge amount of fuel needed to launch the Saturn V (pronounced 'Saturn five') and propel the spacecraft to Earth orbit. This took nearly five hours, throughout the night.

A few days before their mission, Neil, Buzz and Michael spent the night with their families at NASA's secluded beach house near the Kennedy Space Center in Florida.

This time away from the hectic pre-launch schedule allowed the astronauts time for contemplation with their wives and children, ahead of the possibility that they may never return.

The Night before the Launch

The Apollo 11 crew were fully immersed in the meticulously planned pre-launch timetable. Though they were not in quarantine - that came after getting back from the Moon - they did stay overnight at the Manned Spacecraft Operations Building, not far from the administrative headquarters of the Kennedy Space Center, and about eight miles from the launch pad. They revised several procedures before having a meal with friends on Cape Canaveral, where the Kennedy Space Center was situated, having said goodbye to their families the day before. They went to bed at 8.45 pm, getting an early night before the big day.

Neil and Michael in the hallway of the Manned Spacecraft Operations Building before being transported to Launch Complex 39A.

The Morning of the Launch

The astronauts were woken at 4.15 am on launch day, T-5 hours 17 minutes before blast off.

They had a brief medical examination, before settling down to a breakfast of orange juice, steak, scrambled eggs, toast and coffee.

They were joined for breakfast by the Director of Flight Operations, Deke Slayton, who had been an astronaut on NASA's earlier Mercury programme, and Bill Anders, Michael's back-up Command Module pilot.

After breakfast, Neil, Buzz and Michael were helped into their spacesuits by technicians. At 6.27 am, the three astronauts left the Manned Spacecraft Operations Building for the 27 minute drive to Launch Complex 39A, where their spacecraft awaited them.

The photograph on the right shows Neil leading Michael and a technician along Launch Complex 39A as the astronauts make their way to the spacecraft during pre-launch countdown.

"I was certainly aware that this was a culmination of the work of 300,000 or 400,000 people over a decade and that the nation's hopes and outward appearance largely rested on how the results came out. With those pressures, it seemed the most important thing to do was focus on our job as best we were able to and try to allow nothing to distract us from doing the very best job we could. And, you know, I have no complaints about the way my colleagues were able to step up to that." Neil Armstrong

Goodwill messages from around the world brought to the Moon by the astronauts of Apollo 11

'I have great admiration for the skill and perseverance of all those who have contributed to make this first manned flight to the Moon possible. I hope that this achievement will prove of great benefit for the future of mankind.' Queen Juliana, The Netherlands

'The age-old dream of man to cut his bonds to planet Earth and reach for the stars has given him not only wings, but also the intellect and the intrepid spirit which have enabled him to overcome formidable barriers and accomplish extraordinary feats in the exploration of the unknown, culminating in the epochal landing on the Moon.' Ferdinand Marcos, Philippines

'The Government and people of Trinidad and Tobago acclaim this historic triumph of science and the human will. It is our earnest hope for humankind that while we gain the Moon, we shall not lose the world.' Eric Williams, Trinidad and Tobago

'The conquest of the Moon is a glorious milestone along the road of all mankind towards the achievement of peace, freedom and justice.' Giuseppe Saragat, Italy

'Man steps upon the Moon with pride, faith and hope as his inspiration, and peace with progress as his objective.' King Sobhuza II, Swaziland

'Man has reached out and touched the tranquil Moon. May that high accomplishment allow man to rediscover the Earth and find peace.' Pierre Elliott-Trudeau, Canada

From Planet Earth – July 1969

As part of the Apollo 11 mission, a small silicon disk measuring approximately 32 mm in diameter was created to be left on the the Moon, along with the lunar plaque, carrying goodwill messages from Earth. The disk included statements from four American presidents and messages from the leaders of 73 countries from around the world – you can read five of these in the illustration above. Each message was reduced to a size smaller than the head of a pin so that they would all fit on it – the only way they could be read was through a microscope!

Preparing for Lift Off!

Two hours 40 minutes and 40 seconds before launch, Neil, Buzz and Michael boarded the high speed lift. This carried them to the spacecraft 98 metres high at a speedy 180 metres per minute.

Each astronaut carried his own oxygen supply onto the spacecraft, as from the moment they put their spacesuits on, they were sealed off from Earth's natural atmosphere of oxygen and nitrogen. By the time the spacecraft launched, the crew would have been breathing pure oxygen for three hours, with all nitrogen dissolved from their bloodstream. This was essential in preventing nitrogen bubbles forming in their blood due to the low spacecraft air pressure, causing decompression sickness.

Neil and Michael were the first to board the spacecraft. From the lift, they walked along Swing Arm 9, which was the Apollo access arm, to the white room, attached to the spacecraft level. Neil boarded first and was seated in the left hand seat at 6.54 am, followed by Michael shortly afterwards at 6.59 am, sitting in the right hand seat. Buzz, waiting in the lift, boarded the spacecraft at 7.10 am and sat in the middle seat. The astronauts were fitted into the spacecraft by the close-out crew, including Fred Haise, Buzz's backup Lunar Module pilot.

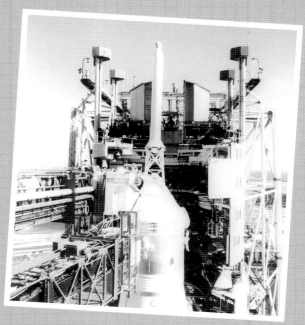

This is the top of the Apollo 11 spacecraft, notably the Command Service Module and part of the Lunar Module. The tower-like feature on top of the spacecraft is the launch escape system, used to quickly separate the crew capsule in case of a launch abort emergency.

The Apollo 11 launch was handled at the Launch Control Center at the Kennedy Space Center in Florida. Once the launch vehicle cleared the launch pad towers, communication was handed over to Mission Control at the Manned Spacecraft Center, now renamed the Johnson Space Center, in Houston, Texas.

Whilst the astronauts were boarding the spacecraft, technicians working at the 61 metre level were tightening bolts around a leaky valve which replenished the hydrogen fuel supply to the third stage of the Saturn V rocket. Had this not been fixed, the Apollo 11 launch could have been delayed for several days!

About an hour before the launch, the close-out crew left the spacecraft, the last people the astronauts would see until splash down eight days later. Five minutes before the launch, Swing Arm 9 swung back from the spacecraft. At T-2 minutes 45 seconds, Saturn V began to pressurise its propellant tanks. This continued for all three stages of the massive launch vehicle right up until the final minute . . .

The World Holds its Breath . . .

On 16 July 1969 at 9.32 am, the Saturn V launched the three astronauts on their epic journey to the Moon.

"T-60 seconds and counting. We've passed T-60. 55 seconds and counting. Neil Armstrong just reported back: 'It's been a real smooth countdown'. We've passed the 50 second mark. Power transfer is complete - we're on internal power with the launch vehicle at this time. 40 seconds away from the Apollo 11 lift off. All the second stage tanks now pressurised. 35 seconds and counting. We are still GO with Apollo 11.

30 seconds and counting.

Astronauts report 'It feels good'.

T-25 seconds, 20 seconds and counting, T-15 seconds, guidance is internal, 12, 11, 10, 9, ignition sequence start, 6, 5, 4, 3, 2, 1, 0, all engines running, lift off!

We have a lift off!

32 minutes past the hour, lift off on Apollo 11!"

This is taken from the transcript of the Mission Control audio as the launch happened.

Here you can see what the view was like for people watching the lift off from the Kennedy Space Center.

How Did They Get to the Moon?

Getting to the Moon required the most advanced machinery ever designed at the time. Each part was essential to land the astronauts on the Moon and return them back home safely.

Command Module

Service Module

Lunar Module

Apollo Spacecraft
(82 Feet High)

Saturn V Launch Vehicle
(281 Feet High)

SATURN V LAUNCH VEHICLE: You need a very powerful rocket to get you all the way to the Moon. The Saturn V had the power to launch ten buses into space. It weighed 2.8 million kilogrammes and measured 281 feet high - that's taller than the Statue of Liberty! The Command Service Module and Lunar Module were attached to the top part of the launch vehicle, as shown in the diagram on the left.

COMMAND MODULE COLUMBIA: Columbia was the main living and working quarters of the Apollo spacecraft for the three astronauts. Inside, it was about the same size as a large car. Can you imagine staying in such cramped conditions with two other people?

SERVICE MODULE: This contained the water, oxygen and electricity used by the astronauts in Columbia. It also held the rocket engine that boosted the spacecraft into lunar orbit and returned it safely to Earth.

LUNAR MODULE EAGLE: The Lunar Module was used to get the astronauts from the Command Service Module to the Moon's surface. The astronauts used it as a base whilst they were on the Moon.

The top part of the Lunar Module could detach itself and was used by Neil and Buzz to return to the spacecraft.

Only the Command Module Columbia survived the mission and returned to Earth. Every other part of the giant launch vehicle and spacecraft was discarded during the mission.

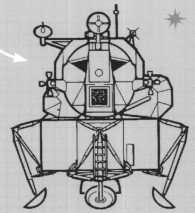

Saturn V Launch Vehicle and Apollo Spacecraft

Command Module - Columbia and Service Module

Lunar Module - Eagle

The Saturn V was one of three types of Saturn rockets built by NASA. Of the two smaller rockets, the Saturn 1B launched humans into Earth orbit, whilst the Saturn 1 was unmanned. The rocket used on the Apollo 11 mission was the sixth Saturn V launch vehicle built for missions going all the way to the Moon. It was made up of three stages to propel the spacecraft beyond Earth orbit. The first stage carried the 770,000 litres of fuel and 1.2 million litres of liquid oxygen needed to ignite the five rocket engines for lift off. At an altitude of 67 km (42 miles), the rocket engines shut down and this first stage fell into the Atlantic Ocean.

The second stage propelled the spacecraft almost to Earth orbit, discarding itself nine minutes and nine seconds after lift off. The third stage had a single rocket engine that was fired until the spacecraft had built up enough speed to reach Earth orbit. 2 1/2 hours later, the engine fired up again to send the astronauts out of Earth orbit. The spacecraft then pulled away from the third stage and continued towards their destination – the Moon!

Blast off! The very moment the Apollo 11 spacecraft launched.

The Command Module was cone shaped and covered in heat shields made from stainless steel honeycomb and epoxy resin. This protected the astronauts from the intense heat experienced during lift off and re-entry. On the bottom of the Service Module was the engine used to push the spacecraft in and out of lunar orbit. This engine also made any adjustments, called 'burns', to ensure that the spacecraft remained on course. These two modules were collectively referred to as the Command Service Module.

The Command and Service Modules being moved onto the Lunar Module in preparation for blast off.

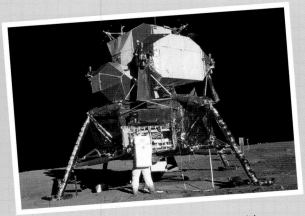
Buzz preparing for experiments on the Moon. Neil took this photograph with a special lunar surface camera.

Unfortunately, you can't see the Eagle at a museum, as the Lunar Module was incapable of re-entering the Earth's atmosphere. The bottom part was left behind on the Moon. The top part returned Buzz and Neil safely to the orbiting Columbia after they had finished exploring, and was then jettisoned into space.

Life on Board

The three astronauts lived in the Command Service Module during the Apollo 11 mission, consisting of the Command Module Columbia and Service Module.

The two modules measured in total 11 metres in length and 3.9 metres maximum diameter. The crew compartment measured approximately 6.17 cubic metres, taking up most of Command Module Columbia, and was where the three astronauts stayed for the eight day mission.

Here you can see detailed diagrams of Columbia's interior. It was divided into three compartments and held a hatch and docking assembly in its tip, enabling the module to connect to the Lunar Module.

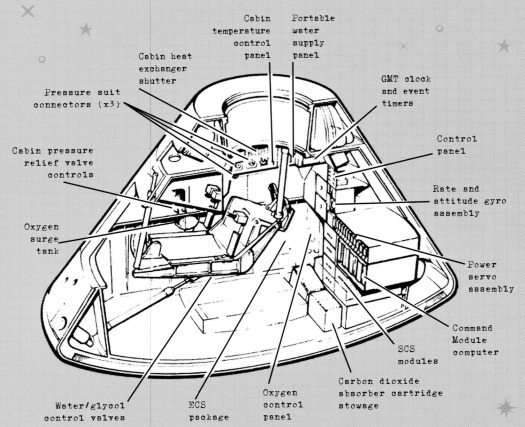

Cabin temperature control panel
Portable water supply panel
Cabin heat exchanger shutter
Pressure suit connectors (x3)
GMT clock and event timers
Control panel
Cabin pressure relief valve controls
Rate and attitude gyro assembly
Oxygen surge tank
Power servo assembly
Command Module computer
SCS modules
Carbon dioxide absorber cartridge stowage
Oxygen control panel
ECS package
Water/glycol control valves

The compartment in the nose of the cone held the equipment required for Earth landing; the one in the base contained reaction control engines, propellant tanks, wiring and plumbing. The crew compartment contained the controls, displays and navigation equipment. The three astronaut couches were lined up in the centre of the crew compartment, with a large access hatch to the side. To provide power after Columbia and the Service Module separated, Columbia held five silver/zinc oxide batteries: three for re-entry and landing, and two for module separation and parachute deployment.

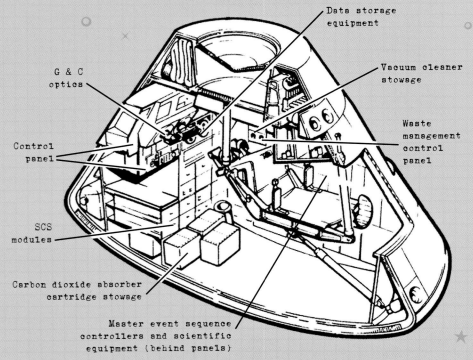

Data storage equipment
Vacuum cleaner stowage
G & C optics
Waste management control panel
Control panel
SCS modules
Carbon dioxide absorber cartridge stowage
Master event sequence controllers and scientific equipment (behind panels)

Did the astronauts sleep and where?

Despite the cramped living quarters and zero gravity environment, all three astronauts were able - in fact required - to stick to a sleeping schedule throughout the mission. Instead of a bed, they slept in sleep restraints - a lightweight zippered sack - which prevented them from floating around in the zero gravity environment of the cabin.

Sleep periods were eight to ten hours on board the spacecraft, with two four to five hour sleep periods for Buzz and Neil on the Eagle incorporated into the lunar surface exploration schedule.

How did they wash or go to the toilet?

The astronauts needed special equipment to stay clean. Shaving foam, razors and an oral hygiene kit were provided. Washing was limited to a sponge bath. To go to the toilet, a urine collection device was worn under their clothing; it was then transferred through a rubber tube and collected in a tank. Poo was collected in a Fecal Collection Bag, which had an adhesive portion for the astronauts to attach to themselves. After use, a germicide was added to prevent bacteria and gas formation, and the bags were sealed and stored in empty food containers for analysis back on Earth.

How did they exercise on board?

In the zero gravity environment of space, exercise is extremely important in order to prevent loss of bone density and muscle wastage. In the confined space of the Columbia, Neil, Buzz and Michael were able to exercise daily using the Exer-Genie Exerciser. Weighing less than one kg and taking up very little room, it was perfect for space travel. The astronauts hooked it on the wall of the Columbia and used it several times a day for periods of 15-30 minutes. By pulling on the cord in a controlled way at varying speeds, they could perform over 100 basic workouts.

What did they do for entertainment?

The astronauts had quite a bit of downtime during their mission, though there was no time allotted for entertainment in the flight plan.

Most of it was spent carrying out on board experiments, navigation checks, exercise, housekeeping and general maintenance of the spacecraft. They also filmed life on board and took amazing photographs of the Moon and planet Earth.

Life on Board: Clothing

The crew had to wear special suits during the mission. They wore lightweight constant wear garments when out of their spacesuits, so that they could be more comfortable whilst on board the spacecraft.

Neil and Buzz wore slightly different spacesuits to Michael, as they were the astronauts leaving the spacecraft to explore the Moon. The spacesuits were known as intravehicular (for inside the spacecraft) and extravehicular (for outside the spacecraft). The two suits were basically identical, apart from the addition of a portable life support system and integrated thermal micrometeroid garment worn over the extravehicular suit. There was a big difference in weight between the two suits: the intravehicular suit weighed 16 kg whilst the extravehicular suit weighed a hefty 83 kg, the weight of an average man. The astronauts tested every item of clothing worn during the mission, from their spacesuits to the biological isolation garment they wore in quarantine after landing. They carried out simulations whilst wearing the spacesuits, enabling them to get used to moving around in the bulky equipment.

In the photos on the right, you can see the various garments being tested by the astronauts and engineers working with NASA.

Biological
Isolation Garment

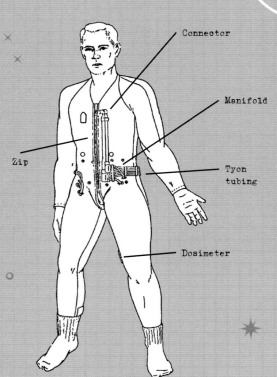

Connector

Manifold

Zip

Tyon tubing

Dosimeter

Liquid Cooling
Garment

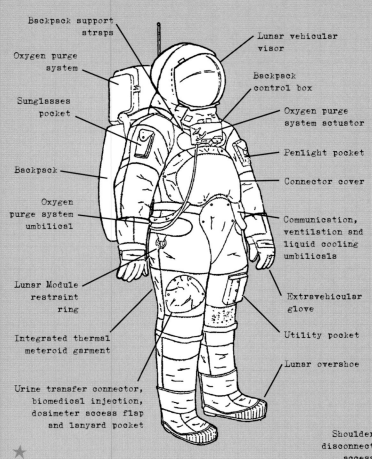

Backpack support straps

Oxygen purge system

Sunglasses pocket

Backpack

Oxygen purge system umbilical

Lunar Module restraint ring

Integrated thermal meteroid garment

Urine transfer connector, biomedical injection, dosimeter access flap and lanyard pocket

Lunar vehicular visor

Backpack control box

Oxygen purge system actuator

Penlight pocket

Connector cover

Communication, ventilation and liquid cooling umbilicals

Extravehicular glove

Utility pocket

Lunar overshoe

THE EXTRAVEHICULAR MOBILITY UNIT (LEFT):
The extravehicular mobility unit provided Buzz and Neil with enough life support for a four hour mission outside the Lunar Module. It was made up of, amongst other elements, the extravehicular suit, integrated thermal micrometeroid garment, liquid cooling garment and portable life support system. The portable life support system (PLSS) was a backpack which supplied oxygen and cooling water for the liquid cooling garment worn by Neil and Buzz when they conducted their Moonwalk.

THE INTEGRATED THERMAL MICROMETEROID GARMENT (BELOW):
This was worn over the top of their extravehicular suits, providing more protection from the lunar temperatures and the possibility of tiny meteoroids hitting them whilst they were outside the lunar module.

THE LIQUID COOLING GARMENT (PICTURED OPPOSITE):
This garment was made of knitted nylon-spandex and was worn under the extravehicular suit and next to the skin. It was worn during exploration outside the Lunar Module instead of the cotton constant wear garment worn on the Command Service Module. This garment circulated cooling water from the PLSS through a network of plastic tubing to keep the astronauts at the right temperature. Even though space is very cold, the extravehicular suit would soon get very hot due to the astronaut's body heat, making body temperature regulation essential for their health.

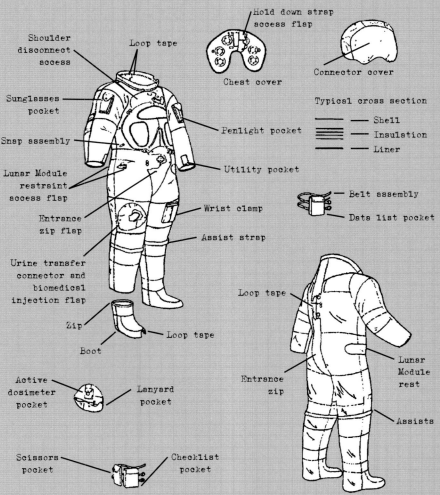

Shoulder disconnect access

Loop tape

Sunglasses pocket

Snap assembly

Lunar Module restraint access flap

Entrance zip flap

Urine transfer connector and biomedical injection flap

Zip

Boot

Active dosimeter pocket

Scissors pocket

Penlight pocket

Utility pocket

Wrist clamp

Assist strap

Loop tape

Lanyard pocket

Checklist pocket

Hold down strap access flap

Chest cover

Connector cover

Typical cross section

———— Shell
≡≡≡≡ Insulation
———— Liner

Belt assembly

Data list pocket

Loop tape

Entrance zip

Lunar Module rest

Assists

Life on Board: Work

Work didn't just start when the astronauts reached the Moon!
Throughout the flight, they had to carry out certain
tasks to ensure that the spacecraft remained on course
and was functioning correctly and safely.

TASK 1: SET THE SPACECRAFT ON COURSE FOR THE MOON

After launch, the spacecraft was temporarily placed into Earth Parking
Orbit. Here, the crew performed various system checks to ensure that the
spacecraft could handle its trip to the Moon. If not, the mission could
be altered to avoid a lunar landing. Checks included the electrical power
system, stabilisation and control system and the crew's biomedical and
safety equipment. When these passed the checks, the Apollo 11 was given
the go-ahead from Mission Control to progress to the Moon.

TASK 2: TRANSLUNAR INJECTION (TLI)

After carrying out system safety checks, the crew fired up the
engine in the third stage rocket for the final time. This extra
boost of power set the spacecraft on the correct trajectory
towards the Moon, a manoeuvre known as translunar injection.

TASK 3: DOCKING WITH LUNAR MODULE

Half an hour after TLI and 3 1/2 hours after lift off, the Command
Service Module was separated from the Saturn V third stage. The
Lunar Module was removed from the Spacecraft Lunar Module Adaptor
(SLA), in which it was stored, turned around and attached (called
'docking') with the Command Service Module.

TASK 4: TRANSLUNAR COAST PHASE

The spacecraft did not need fuel to reach the Moon 380,000 km away.
There is no air resistance in space due to the lack of atmosphere, so the
spacecraft coasted away from Earth, the Earth's gravity slowing it down.
When the Moon's gravitational pull was greater than the Earth's, it began
to speed up again. This was known as the translunar coast phase. The
spacecraft did, however, make intermittent midcourse correction burns -
a technical way of saying firing the engine - to improve the accuracy
at which the spacecraft passed around the far side of the Moon.

TASK 5: PREPARING FOR DESCENT

The astronauts still had over 20 hours to get to the Moon at this
point. Throughout the rest of the flight, they continued to carry out
further checks and on board preparations to make sure that everything
was working properly before beginning the descent.

This photograph shows the view of Earth from the
Apollo 11 spacecraft following translunar injection.

"Houston. Apollo 11. The earthshine coming through
the window is so bright you could read a book by it."
Michael Collins

Life on Board: Food

You are a long way from a supermarket in space, so all meals take a lot of planning before a mission. The three astronauts on the Apollo 11 chose their menus, consisting of three meals a day, well before going into space.

Eating in space has changed a lot over the years. If you asked the question, "How do astronauts eat in space?" at the time of the Apollo 11 mission, the answer would be very different than it is today. When astronauts first went to the Moon, they ate food from dehydrated pouches prepared in a kitchen on Earth before the mission. Most of the food was freeze-dried and the astronauts simply had to add water to the pouch and knead it a few times to make it ready to eat. Once the food was ready, they snipped off the end of the pouch and squeezed it into their mouths. Today, astronauts eat their meals in the same way as they do here on Earth.

The Apollo 11 crew had less food choices than astronauts today. Even so, the range of menu choices that Neil, Buzz and Michael had might still surprise you! They could choose from food as diverse as shrimp cocktail, cornflakes and butterscotch pudding.

Cooks at the astronaut quarters of the NASA Kennedy Space Center preparing meals for the Apollo 11 astronauts a few days before their mission.

DID YOU KNOW?

- Sliced bread is banned in space as the crumbs can float around and damage equipment.

- Astronauts prefer spicy food. Rising body fluids due to microgravity cause congestion, so only strong flavours can be tasted properly.

- The first food eaten in space was caviar and meat pâté, by Russian cosmonaut (and first man in space) Yuri Gagarin in 1961.

- Fizzy drinks are banned as they can cause 'wet burping'. Due to microgravity, any gas in your stomach does not rise to the top but stays mixed with the food, causing you to vomit whenever you burp.

- Every space meal is nutritionally balanced to provide the astronauts with everything they need to keep them healthy in space.

These are examples of food packets used on the Gemini-3 space flight in March 1965 which are similar to those eaten on the Apollo 11 mission.

They include dehydrated beef pot roast, bacon and egg bites, toasted bread cubes, orange juice and a wet wipe. Water is being inserted into the pouch of dehydrated beef pot roast.

Neil, Michael and Buzz eating breakfast with Deke Slayton, NASA's director of flight crew operations, on launch day.

Although their food choices were limited, the astronauts did get to choose what they ate for each day on board. On the right hand side of this page, you will see a list of their food choices. They ate three meals a day and below you can see what Buzz Aldrin ate on Day 3 of the mission:

MEAL A

Peaches
Bacon squares (8)
Apricot cereal cubes (4)
Grape drink
Orange drink

MEAL B

Cream of chicken soup
Turkey and gravy
Cheese cracker cubes (5)
Chocolate cubes (6)
Pineapple-grapefruit
drink

MEAL C

Tuna salad
Chicken stew
Butterscotch pudding
Cocoa
Grapefruit drink

LIST OF FOOD ON BOARD .... Units

BREAKFAST
Peaches	6
Fruit cocktail	6
Canadian bacon and applesauce	3
Bacon squares (8)	12
Sausage patties	3
Sugar coated corn flakes	6
Strawberry cubes (4)	3
Cinnamon toasted bread cubes (4)	6
Apricot cereal cubes (4)	3
Peanut cubes (4)	3

SALADS/MEATS
Salmon salad	3
Tuna salad	3
Cream of chicken soup	6
Shrimp cocktail	6
Spaghetti and meat sauce	6
Beef pot roast	3
Beef and vegetables	3
Chicken and rice	6
Chicken stew	3
Beef stew	3
Pork and scalloped potatoes	6
Ham and potatoes	3
Turkey and gravy	6

REHYDRATABLE DESSERTS
Banana pudding	6
Butterscotch pudding	6
Applesauce	6
Chocolate pudding	6

BEVERAGES
Orange drink	6
Orange-grapefruit drink	3
Pineapple-grapefruit drink	3
Grapefruit drink	3
Grape drink	6
Grape punch	3
Cocoa	6
Coffee	45

DRIED FRUITS
Apricots	6
Peaches	6
Pears	6

SANDWICH SPREAD
Ham salad (5 oz)	1
Tuna salad (5 oz)	1
Chicken salad (5 oz)	1
Cheddar cheese (2 oz)	3

BREAD
Rye	6
White	6

BITES
Cheese cracker cubes (6)	6
BBQ beef bites (4)	6
Chocolate cubes (4)	6
Brownies (4)	6
Date fruitcake (4)	6
Pineapple fruitcake (4)	6
Jellied fruit candy (4)	6
Caramel candy	6

Preparing to Land on the Moon

75 hours 50 minutes into the mission, the service propulsion system (SPS) fired up to push the spacecraft into an initial elliptical lunar orbit. 'Elliptical' means non-circular - the spacecraft began orbiting the Moon in an egg-shape.

Two revolutions later, a second burn (or firing) of the SPS adjusted the spacecraft's lunar orbit. This second burn was carried out to circularise the orbit of the spacecraft following the initial burn of the SPS, which had placed Apollo 11 in an elliptical orbit around the Moon. Both lunar orbit insertion burns took place when the spacecraft was behind the Moon and out of satellite range. It must have been a tense time waiting for news back at Mission Control!

The spacecraft orbited the Moon several times after entering lunar orbit. The astronauts saw passing views of the Lunar Module's landing site in the southern Sea of Tranquility. This area had been chosen due to its relatively smooth surface, as identified by automated spacecraft sent to scout out possible landing sites for a manned lunar landing.

19 hours 30 minutes after lunar orbit insertion, Neil and Buzz entered Lunar Module Eagle. The Lunar Module had been extracted from the Spacecraft Lunar Module Adaptor immediately after the third stage burn three days earlier had pushed the spacecraft out of Earth orbit and on its way to the Moon.

The Lunar Module descent propulsion system placed the Eagle in orbit at a low point above the Moon of 50,000 feet. From here, the descent and touchdown on the Moon's surface could be made.

Above: This is a detailed view of the far side of the Moon in the vicinity of Crater No. 308.

Left: This is an interior view of the Lunar Module. In it, you can see some of the displays and controls.

The Descent

The Eagle, carrying Buzz and Neil, began its descent to the Moon's surface on the fifth day of the Apollo 11 mission. This is shown in this photograph taken by Michael. He piloted the Command Service Module in a parking orbit around the Moon whilst the other two astronauts explored the surface. As well as taking photographs, Michael also checked the Eagle for damage as it hung below him in space.

The Lunar Module's descent was a tense time for the crews both in space and back on Earth. Neil and Buzz reported to Mission Control that they were passing landmarks on the Moon's surface four seconds earlier than anticipated. This meant that they would land a few miles west of their primary landing site in a rocky area close to a 400 metre diameter crater.

When Mission Control had given the GO for landing, a series of programme alarms and low fuel warnings caused more alarm. Neil took semi-automatic control of the Lunar Module in order to find a reasonably smooth place to land in the Sea of Tranquility. They thought that they had only 30 seconds of fuel remaining,

though post-flight analysis found this to be a misreading by the system. They actually had almost twice that hover time remaining!

NEIL ARMSTRONG:
"Houston, Tranquility Base here. The Eagle has landed."

MISSION CONTROL:
"Roger, Tranquility. We copy you on the ground. You got a bunch of guys about to turn blue. We're breathing again. Thanks a lot."

The view of the landing site, taken from the Lunar Module whilst in orbit.

109 hours 24 minutes after launch, at 10.56 pm EDT on 20 July 1969, the Lunar Module hatch opened and Neil climbed down the ladder. As he stepped onto the Moon, he made his famous announcement: "That's one small step for [a] man, one giant leap for mankind." Buzz followed 20 minutes later. He described the lunar surface as "Magnificent desolation".

Neil and Buzz explored the Moon for 2 1/2 hours, during which time they carried out experiments and collected samples of lunar materials. They also set up a United States flag and laid a plaque commemorating the successful Moon landing. A television camera on the Lunar Module was able to record what they were doing and they also took photographs. The astronaut you see in the photos on these pages is Buzz. There are a couple of panoramic photos of Neil on the Moon, but no posed images as he was the person behind the camera. The astronauts spent 21 hours 37 minutes on the Moon but most of that time was spent in the Lunar Module. Here, they rested and performed system checks before being launched back up to the Command Service Module.

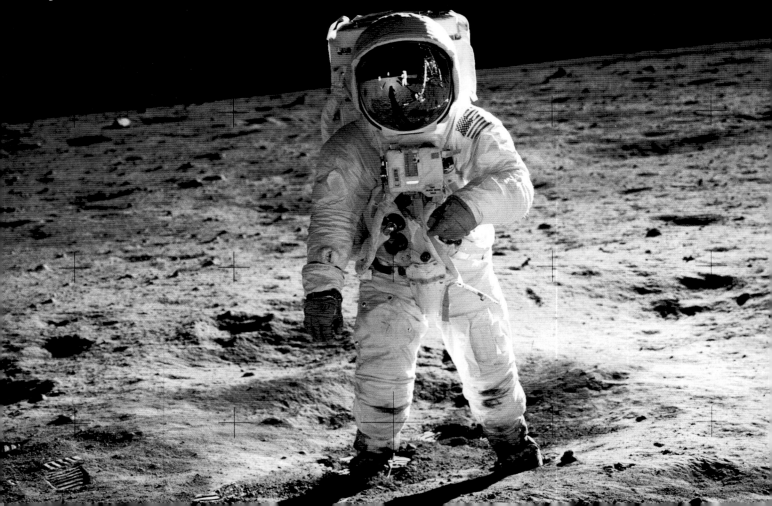

Bulk and Core Sample Collections

Neil and Buzz collected 22 kg of lunar surface material. This consisted of 50 rocks and samples of lunar soil. Two core samples from 13 cm below the Moon's surface were taken with a tube knocked into the ground with a hammer.

The rocks and samples were sealed and analysed at the Manned Spacecraft Center's Lunar Receiving Laboratory back in Houston. After the mission, a small amount of Moon rock was given to 135 countries on Earth in a gesture of goodwill.

Here, Buzz is using the core sampler to collect samples from below the Moon's surface.

In the photograph on the left you can see a close up of lunar rocks collected by Neil and Buzz.

To the right is a magnified photograph of a lunar rock sample. It contains the minerals ilmenite and pyroxene.

Scientific Experiments

The astronauts carried out two basic experiments known collectively as the Early Apollo Scientific Experiments Package (EASEP). Both experiments were held in individual packages weighing a total of around 77 kg. The EASEP also contained the Lunar Dust Detector, which measured the effects of Moon dust on the two experiments.

The Passive Seismic Experiment Package (PSEP) measured vibrations caused by meteoroid impacts and Moonquakes. This experiment provided information to help us learn more about the internal structure of the Moon and how similar or dissimilar it is to the Earth's interior. The Laser Ranging Retro-Reflector (LRRR) was used to measure the precise distance between the Earth and the Moon. It consisted of a set of 100 reflectors set into a pallet of 0.45 square metres and aligned with Earth. Pulses of laser light transmitted from Earth to the Moon were reflected back to Earth, accurately measuring the distance. The LRRR has been continuously in operation since Neil and Buzz set it up in 1969 and is still in use today!

In this photo, Buzz prepares to set up the Early Apollo Scientific Experiments Package on the surface of the Moon.

Here, you can see the plaque that the astronauts left on the Moon to commemorate the mission.

TV Transmission

NASA had to use a special slow-scan Lunar Camera for the transmission of the famous television images from the Moon. The camera was kept in the Lunar Module's descent stage storage area on the right of the ladder. Neil released this by pulling a lanyard which unfolded the tray holding the camera. This captured him going down the ladder of the Lunar Module before taking the historic first steps on the Moon.

The Lunar Module had an antenna which could transmit the television signal to one of the tracking stations back on Earth. Many tracking stations were needed around the world because the Earth rotates and there always had to be a tracking station in line with the Moon to receive the television signal. The tracking station receiving the images of Neil taking his first steps on the Moon was located in Australia. The signals were relayed from the tracking station which received the transmission, to Mission Control in Houston, who then broadcast the footage to the world.

Here, Buzz is setting up the Passive Seismic Experiment Package.

In this photograph, Buzz poses in front of the United States flag. On the opposite page you can see Buzz working on the Solar Wind Composition experiment. Behind him is the Lunar Module.

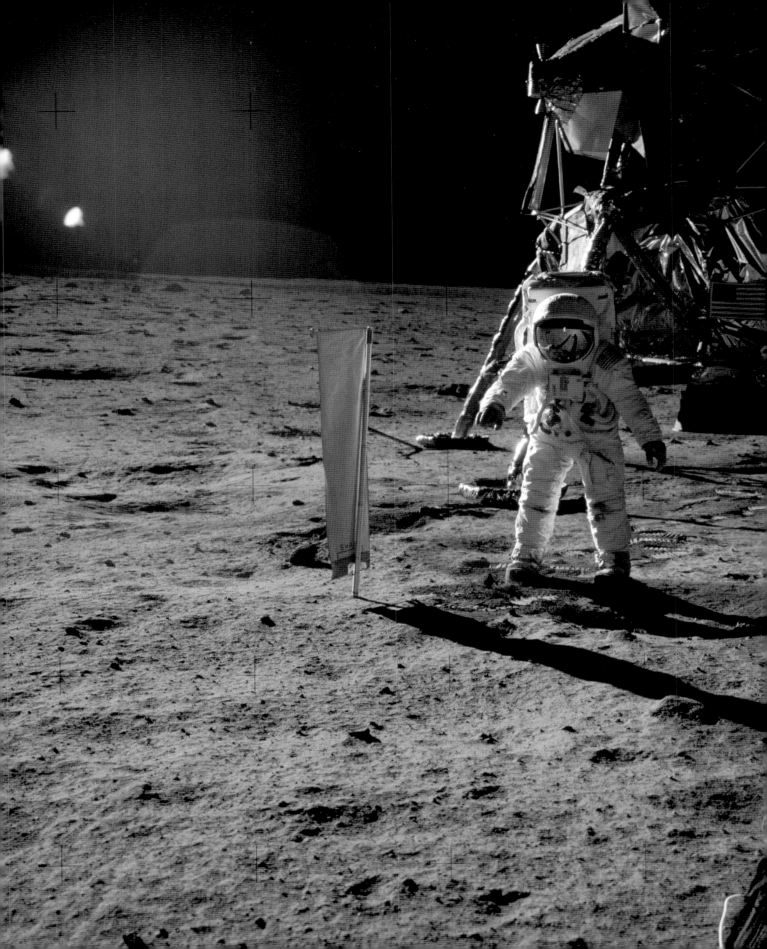

What was Michael Doing?

Michael spent nearly 28 hours alone in lunar orbit on board Command Module Columbia. With Buzz and Neil down on the Moon's surface and the world's population back on planet Earth, he was described as the 'loneliest person in the universe' during this time.

Michael had flown in space before — on NASA's earlier Gemini X mission — completed in 1966.

Michael orbited the Moon alone for nearly 28 hours. Contact with Earth was abruptly cut off each time he passed the far side, as there were no satellites to transmit his radio messages, leaving him completely alone.

Michael grew very fond of Columbia. After returning to Earth, he wrote a tribute to the spacecraft, describing it as "The best ship to come down the line."

During his time alone in lunar orbit, Michael ran system checks on the spacecraft, performed Moon observations and kept in contact with Mission Control. Despite not walking on the Moon, Michael was an integral part of the mission. Attempting to land on the Moon is a highly dangerous operation with lots of risk involved - and there was a high possibility that Neil and Buzz could remain stranded on the Moon. Part of Michael's job was to help them get back to the Command Service Module safely.

"The thing I remember most is the view of planet Earth from a great distance: tiny, very shiny, blue and white, bright, very beautiful, serene and fragile." Michael Collins

What if Things Went Wrong?

The Apollo space programme used new technology to explore the unknown, with a high risk of loss of life. Despite all preparations and tests done back on Earth, no one could be sure what exactly would happen once the astronauts entered deep space.

In 1967, Apollo 1, the first Apollo mission, ended in tragedy: all three astronauts lost their lives in a fire during a routine test. This fire was caused by the 100% oxygen atmosphere in the cabin, a condition that, though necessary to sustain life whilst in orbit, is highly flammable. The disaster reminded NASA just how risky space exploration was and led to a complete overhaul of their safety measures. Apollo 11 had several abort modes and alternate missions in place in case something went wrong. As well as equipment failure, one of the major worries was a lack of fuel to boost the spacecraft in and out of Earth and lunar orbit. There was the very real possibility that the Lunar Module would not blast off from the Moon, leaving Neil and Buzz stranded, never to return home. In this scenario, a contingency plan was prepared: President Nixon would telephone Buzz and Neil's wives before making the televised speech you can see on the right. When NASA ended communication with the doomed astronauts, a clergyman would follow the same process as a burial at sea. Fortunately, the mission was a success and the contingency plan never needed!

Fate has ordained that the men who went to the Moon to explore in peace will stay on the Moon to rest in peace. These brave men, Neil Armstrong and Edwin Aldrin, know that there is no hope for their recovery. But they also know that there is hope for mankind in their sacrifice. These two men are laying down their lives in mankind's most noble goal: the search for truth and understanding. They will be mourned by their families and friends; they will be mourned by their nation; they will be mourned by the people of the world; they will be mourned by a Mother Earth that dared send two of her sons into the unknown. In their exploration, they stirred the people of the world to feel as one; in their sacrifice, they bind more tightly the brotherhood of man. In ancient days, men looked at stars and saw their heroes in the constellations. In modern times, we do much the same, but our heroes are epic men of flesh and blood. Others will follow, and surely find their way home. Man's search will not be denied. But these men were the first, and they will remain the foremost in our hearts. For every human being who looks up at the Moon in the nights to come will know that there is some corner of another world that is forever mankind.

Here you can see President Nixon (right) watching and waiting nervously for the Apollo 11 crew to land safely back to Earth.

The Ascent and Docking

After exploring the surface of the Moon, Neil and Buzz
returned to the Lunar Module Eagle for a rest period
before returning to the Columbia orbiting above them.
This included seven hours of sleep and time to fully
prepare for blast off from the Moon.

The Lunar Module consisted of two sections: the ascent stage and the
descent stage. The two astronauts flew in the ascent stage for their
rendezvous with the spacecraft, using the descent stage as a launch pad.

This was a tense time for the crews in space and Mission Control, as no
one was certain that there would be enough fuel for lift off. Fortunately,
124 hours 22 minutes into the mission, the ascent stage engine fired,
beginning the ascent back to Columbia in lunar orbit.

The engine stopped firing once the Lunar Module ascent stage reached
lunar orbit, 44 nautical miles (18.3 km) above the Moon. Smaller
engines were fired up for two course correction burns during the
journey, to keep the ascent stage in line with the orbiting
Command Service Module.

About 3 1/2 hours after blasting off from Tranquility Base, the Lunar
Module ascent stage docked with the Command Service Module. This means
that the two modules were reattached. Neil and Buzz returned to the
Command Module, reuniting them with Michael after their adventure
on the Moon.

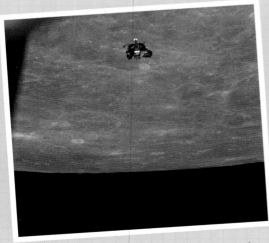

Here you can see the Lunar Module during the
ascent stage photographed by Michael from
the Command Service Module.

The Lunar Module ascent stage was
unable to survive re-entry to the
Earth's atmosphere. Four hours
after Neil and Buzz returned to
the spacecraft, the astronauts
jettisoned the Lunar Module into
space. It eventually collided with
the Moon due to lunar gravity.

Shortly afterwards, the spaceship
was placed in transEarth coast
and the astronauts began their
journey home.

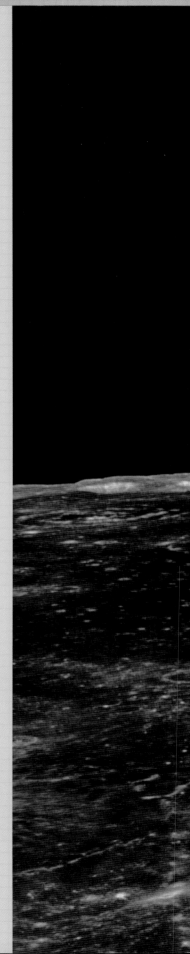

"I was intensely aware of the importance of this phase of the mission. There was no turning back, and this was the only way to pick up the astronauts. There were hundreds of things that could go wrong, at any second. And, each step without a problem brought us closer to success. It took about two hours from lift off to get to the position to dock with the orbiting Command Module. The step of docking was a big one and brings us that much closer to final success. Docking came in due time and the crew moved to the Command Module. There was a strong feeling of gratitude and affection towards that small Lunar Module when it was jettisoned. We could now get the crew into the familiar Command Module and start the preps to fire the engine to get back to Earth. We felt blessed and thankful that all went well and the crew was on its way back home." Glynn S. Lunney, officer on duty in Mission Control at the Kennedy Space Center, 1969

Fantastic Lunar Facts!

The Moon has its own set of regions and landmarks just like a country
on Earth. Though NASA does not have the authority to formally name landmarks
on the Moon, informal names were assigned during the Apollo missions.
Below you can find information about some lunar landmarks.

THE APOLLO BASIN - a 540 km (335.5 miles)
diameter crater on the southwestern far side,
named in honour of the Apollo missions.

ARISTARCHUS CRATER - this is named after the
ancient Greek astronomer Aristarchus of Samos.
It is the brightest feature on the side of the
Moon visible on Earth. That is because it is
estimated to have only been formed within the
last billion years - recent in lunar terms!

FAR SIDE OF THE MOON - this is the side of the
Moon that always faces away from planet Earth.
The surface is rugged and covered with impact
craters and relatively few lunar seas. It is
also known as the 'dark side', though this is
not entirely accurate - over one lunar orbit
of the Earth, the far side of the Moon receives
just as much sunlight as the near side.

MOUNT MARILYN - a lunar mountain separating
the Sea of Tranquility from the Sea of
Fertility. Originally called Secchi Theta,
it was informally named in 1968 by astronaut
Jim Lovell after his wife, Marilyn. This name
was officially recognised in 2017.

TSIOLKOVSKY - a large lunar impact crater named
after Russian scientist Konstantin Tsiolkovsky.
It is located in the southern hemisphere on the
far side of the Moon.

TYCHO - a 85 km (52.8 miles) diameter lunar
crater named after Danish astronomer Tycho Brahe.
It is located in the southern lunar highland and
is estimated to be 108 million years old.

SEA OF MOSCOW - a lunar sea that sits in the
Moscoviense basin on the far side of the Moon.
It is one of the very few seas on the far side
and is named after the Russian scientists who
first mapped it.

SEA OF SHOWERS - also called the 'Sea of
Rains'. It is a 1,145 km (711.5 miles) diameter
lava plain in the Imbrium Basin. It is one of
the largest craters in the known Solar System.

SEA OF TRANQUILITY - this is a lunar sea found
in the Tranquillitatis Basin. It was chosen as
the landing site for the Apollo 11 due to its
relatively smooth surface.

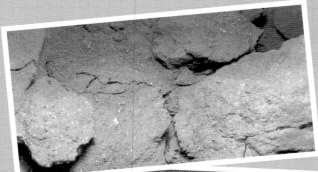

These are photographs of the lunar surface taken by Neil and Buzz
during their Moonwalk. The top image shows a close up of lunar surface
powder and the bottom image the surface of a lunar rock.

Did you know?

- Despite their names, lunar seas are not actually filled with liquid. They are in fact areas of solidified lava which appear dark on the Moon's surface. Many are large enough for you to see with your own eyes, without the need for a telescope.

- There is an estimated 181,437 kg of man-made materials left on the Moon from Apollo missions. Some have been photographed by space probes.

- The Moon is gradually moving away from the Earth. It drifts approximately 3.8 cm further away every year. That's about the same rate at which your fingernails grow!

"That's one small step for [a] man, one giant leap for mankind," was unscripted. Neil had the time from landing the Lunar Module to descending the ladder to think of a statement in keeping with NASA's official viewpoint and his own feelings. His iconic quote is the result. Here you can see Buzz about to take his first step on the Moon, photographed by Neil.

- Although Neil and Buzz raised a United States flag on the Moon, no one country is allowed to claim the Moon as its own territory. The Outer Space Treaty, signed in 1967, prevents possible damage to the Moon by banning military activity in space.

- The average surface temperature on the Moon is 107 degrees Celsius during the day, dropping to a chilly -153 degrees Celsius at night.

- The Moon has a very thin atmosphere, so there is no wind to blow the layer of Moon dust on the surface. As such, the footprints left by Apollo astronauts will probably remain undisturbed for centuries.

- The Moon, along with the Sun, are responsible for high and low tides. The Moon's gravitational force pulls up water on the side of the Earth facing it, with water on the other side of Earth pulling in the opposite direction. As the Earth rotates, the result is a high and low tide twice a day.

- The Moon may have helped create life on Earth. Its gravitational pull stabilised Earth's tilt, leading to the stable environment needed for life to thrive.

We would like to thank Ralph Timberlake, Nathan Trail, Gill Norman, Jenny Heller and everyone at the British Interplanetary Society for their help in making this book possible. Special thanks also go to Helen Sharman, Chris Petty, David Baker and Imogen Tomlinson.

The British Interplanetary Society (BIS) promotes the exploration and use of space for the benefit of humanity, by connecting people to create, educate and inspire, and advance knowledge in all aspects of astronautics.

The BIS is Britain's leading think tank on space development. Founded in 1933, it is the world's longest established organisation devoted solely to supporting and promoting the exploration of space and astronautics.

The BIS is devoted to initiating, promoting and disseminating new concepts and technical information about space flight and astronautics through meetings, symposia, publications, visits and exhibitions.

For more information visit www.bis-space.com

All imagery and photographs printed in this book are from the NASA Image and Video Library (unless stated otherwise below). For more information visit www.nasa.gov

BLAST OFF TO THE MOON is a uclanpublishing book

First published in Great Britain in 2019 by uclanpublishing
in association with the British Interplanetary Society
University of Central Lancashire, Preston, PR1 2HE, UK